A love-and-laughter
gift to you
from
♥ the Geranium Lady

And me, ♥

_____

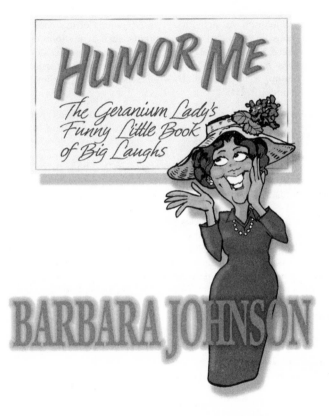

HUMOR ME

The Geranium Lady's Funny Little Book of Big Laughs

BARBARA JOHNSON

Guideposts®

CARMEL, NEW YORK 10512

This Guideposts edition is published by special arrangement with Thomas Nelson Publishers.

Unless otherwise indicated, Scripture quotations used in this book are from the New Century Version (NCV) © 1987, 1988, 1991 by Word Publishing, Nashville, Tennessee 37214. Used by permission.

Other quotations are from the New American Standard Bible (NASB) © 1960, 1962, 1963, 1968, 1971, 1972, 1973, 1975, 1977 by the Lockman Foundation, La Habra, California. All rights reserved.

Unless noted, the sources of the stories, jokes, and quips included in this volume are unknown, and the author claims no rights or ownership. Many have been contributed as unidentified published or Internet clippings, and although attempts have been made to identify the material's origin, in many cases this was impossible. Some of the material in *Humor Me* has previously appeared in the author's earlier books published by Word Publishing and W Publishing Group.

Cover art by Dennis Hill.

Library of Congress Cataloging-in-Publication Data

Johnson, Barbara.
   Humor me / by Barbara Johnson.
      p. cm.
   ISBN 0-8499-1787-5 (hardcover)
   1. American wit and humor.   I. Title.
PN6165.J64 2003
818'.02—dc21

2003001061

Printed in the United States of America

CONTENTS

HUMOR COMES AT A COST.
PLEASE HAVE EXACT CHANGE

If you can find the humor hidden in a daunting day . . . you can survive it

*L*aughing is my favorite aerobic exercise (right after breathing and eating), and *shared* laughter is my favorite form of fun. This little volume is packed full of my favorite exercise routines: jokes, quips, and cartoons that take me anywhere from giggle to guffaw. Come along, and we'll chuckle our way to being "humorically fit" together. (A friend of mine who's into football calls this my "playbook," and it's a perfect title, because I especially love to laugh while I'm playing!)

Just thinking about all the funny things God put on this earth makes me chuckle. In this book we'll look at some of the most laughable: the wonders of womanhood, the thrill and terror of child rearing, the Catch-22 of aging, the mirthful mysteries of men, and that hilarious show-stopper: death.

Maybe you bought this book simply because you love to laugh, too. Or maybe you picked it up because you've hit a pothole on your life's journey that has knocked the joy right out of you. Or this book might have been a gift from someone who thinks you could use a few laps around the laugh track right now. This collection of nonsense is designed to realign your sense of humor, energize your joy level, and shine a little fun-light into your life.

No matter when or where you find it, laughter is always good for you. But its benefits seem most powerful when we laugh because we *need* to, and its therapeutic effects are greatly enhanced when we (finally) laugh again because someone who loves us helps us remember how. It might happen at a pink-slip point in our lives. Or a door-slamming junction of some sorts. Or it might even come after we've taken one of those long, lonely trips to the cemetery in the car following the hearse.

When life is easy, humor sparkles like diamonds on the smooth surface of the sea. When life is hard, humor is the life jacket that keeps us from going under. Whatever the conditions are on *your* part of life's ocean right now, I hope the humor in this little book will fill your sails with gales of encouragement and laughter.

❀

A woman called the utility company and complained that her electricity was out. "What should I do?" she asked.

The voice on the other end advised, "Open your freezer and eat the ice cream."[1]

❀

A greeting-card line you'll never see:
I'm so miserable without you,
it's almost like you're here.

❀

When small decisions have major consequences . . .

When trouble arises and things look bad, there is always one individual who perceives a solution and is willing to take command. Very often, that person is crazy.

—DAVE BARRY

❀

Warning signs that you've *really* reached the end of your rope:

- You don't worry when the wind blows, because you don't have anything left to blow away.
- Your dog follows someone else home.
- You can't even afford tuition for the school of hard knocks.
- You've kept a stiff upper lip so long that rigor mortis has set in.

❀

A conscience is what hurts when
all your other parts feel so good.

❀

Kinder, gentler ways to indicate stupidity:

- She's a few peas short of a casserole.
- His antenna doesn't pick up all the channels.
- Her phone's permanently off the hook.
- His belt doesn't go through all the loops.
- Her Slinky's permanently kinked.
- In his brain, the wheel's spinning, but the hamster's dead.

❀

When one door closes, another door always opens—
but those long hallways in between are a real drag.[2]

❀

A little boy and his grandmother were walking along
the seashore when a monstrous wave appeared out of
nowhere and swept the child out to sea. The grandmother, horrified, fell to her knees and said, "God,
please return my beloved grandson. Please, I beg of
You. Send him back safely."

Suddenly another huge wave came rolling in and
deposited the little boy on the sand at her feet. She
picked him up and looked him over, then she looked up
at the sky and said, "He had a hat!"[3]

❀

MOTHER GOOSE AND GRIMM • By Mike Peters

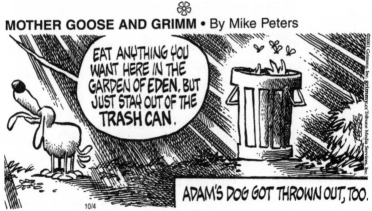

❀

It may be that your sole purpose in life is
simply to serve as a warning to others.

❀

Light travels faster than sound. This is why some
people appear bright until you hear them speak.

❀

Those who insist on keeping an orderly home will
never know the thrilling sense of glee at finding something they thought was lost forever.

❀

Those to whom I can't relate
I'm proud to say are few.
But I wonder why it is that they
Are those I'm related to.

❀

Maybe that's why . . . a family reunion is the most
effective form of birth control.

❀

Like the sundial . . .
I resolve to count only
the sunny hours!

❀

If you can't be kind,
at least have the decency to be vague.

❀

**Life is an adventure. Hang on to your hat
and scream for all you're worth!**

❀

Life's a journey, and it comes with heavy baggage;
laughter's the porter who helps us carry the cargo.

❀

There will be no crises next week.
My schedule is already full.

❀

Laughter is a tranquilizer with no side effects.

❀

The rain falls on the just and also on the unjust,
But chiefly on the just,
Because the unjust steals the just's umbrella.

❀

The colder the x-ray table, the more of your body is required to be on it.

—STEVEN WRIGHT

❀

You can turn painful situations around through laughter. If you can find humor in anything—even poverty—you can survive it.

—BILL COSBY

❀

Real letters to Action Line:
- "The directions on my hair conditioner say to squeeze excess water from hair and shake well before using, but it gives me a headache to shake my head that hard."
- "Do any of the mortuaries around here have cremation? If so, can you manage to get it before you die to make sure you have it?"
- "Once a week I bowl with the girls. Do I burn up enough calories to eat a sundae afterwards?"[4]

❀

If at first you *do* succeed . . .
try not to look astonished.

❀

Human beings can live without air for a few minutes, without water for a week, without food for six weeks, . . . and without a new thought for a lifetime!

❀

ZIGGY   **By Tom Wilson**

❀

There are three kinds of people:
Those who can count and those who can't.

❀

Being "well adjusted" means you can make the same mistakes over and over again—and keep smiling.

❀

You are a child of God. Call home.

❀

What to do in case of fire:

During a recent ecumenical gathering a secretary rushed in shouting, "The building is on fire!"

The Methodists hurriedly gathered in a corner and prayed.

The Baptists cried, "Where's the water?"

The Quakers quietly praised God for the blessings that fire brings.

The Lutherans posted a notice on the door declaring the fire was evil.

The Roman Catholics passed the plate to cover the damage.

The Jews posted symbols on the doors hoping the fire would pass.

The Congregationalists shouted, "Every man for himself!"

The Fundamentalists proclaimed, "It's the vengeance of God!"

The Episcopalians formed a procession and marched out.

The Christian Scientists concluded that there was no fire.

The Presbyterians appointed a chairperson who was to appoint a committee to look into the matter and submit a written report.

The secretary grabbed the fire extinguisher and put out the fire.

❈

Don't let people drive you crazy
when you know insanity is within walking distance.

❈

Everyone's heard of the Twelve Step program, but there's also a remarkable ONE step program: "*WHAM! Get over it!*"

❈

She who waters others will also be watered herself.
(Proverbs 11:25 adapted)

❀

Medical definitions from the Home for the Bewildered:

Clinical depression: The print your behind makes on the doctor's examination table.

Bonding: What chewing gum does between your shoe and the pavement.

Repressing: What you'll be doing to your pants after a thirteen-hour car trip.

Healing process: Teaching your dog to walk beside you.

—SHERRIE WEAVER

❀

Practical guide for successful living:
Put your head under the pillow and scream.

❀

Church signs that made me smile:

- God grades on the cross, not on the curve.
- Exposure to the Son may prevent burning!
- God loves everyone but probably prefers "fruits of the Spirit" over "religious nuts"!

❀

As she left church, the old lady shook hands with the minister and said, "Thank you for your sermon. It was like water to a drowning man."[5]

❀

My doctor is an eye, ear, nose, throat,
and wallet specialist.[6]

❀

Overheard in a doctor's office:
"I've been waiting so long, I think I've recovered!"

❀

Money talks. Most often mine says good-bye.

❀

The youngest children enrolled in a church preschool always steal the show at the annual Christmas program. Last year the children—none of whom could yet read—held up brightly colored three-foot-high cards that spelled out Christmas words. The highlight came when one foursome walked onstage in reverse order and proudly spelled **RATS.**

❀

God's promises are like the stars.
The darker the night, the brighter they shine.[7]

❀

ZIGGY   **By Tom Wilson**

❀

Now you are sad, but I will see you again and you will be happy, and no one will take away your joy.

JOHN 16:22

I FINALLY GOT MY HEAD TOGETHER—
THEN MY BODY FELL APART

I'm not fat . . . I'm calorically gifted

Ah, the joys of womanhood! In this chapter we'll celebrate all the things that make us unique (and, occasionally, make us crazy), from dieting to driving. As we juggle challenging careers, worrisome health issues, and exhausting family demands (from tending husbands and corralling kids to refereeing sibling disagreements to helping aging parents), we sometimes want to hang a sign on our lives like the note posted on a harried shopkeeper's door:

> Out of my mind.
> Be back in five minutes.

Come along for the fun. If we're stumbling toward the Home for the Bewildered, we might as well laugh as we go.

❀

Amazing! You just hang something in your closet for a while, and it shrinks two sizes.

❀

SIX CHICKS

Things you got from your mother.

❀

Every now and then, without warning, each of us has a good day.

Please, Lord, let today be my day!

❀

Only *some* of us learn by other people's mistakes. The rest of us have to be the other people.

❀

Enjoy the little things in life.

One day you may look back and realize they were the big things.

❀

A lady shopping at a big discount store put several items in her cart then headed for the checkout counter. There she learned that one of her items would not scan, so the man running the cash register couldn't tell what the price was. Imagine her embarrassment when he got on the store's public address system and boomed out for all the shoppers to hear: "PRICE CHECK ON LANE THIRTEEN. TAMPAX. SUPER SIZE."

That was bad enough, but the guy at the rear of the store apparently misunderstood the word "Tampax" for "THUMBTACKS." In a businesslike tone, his voice boomed back: "DO YOU WANT THE KIND YOU PUSH IN WITH YOUR THUMB OR THE KIND YOU POUND IN WITH A HAMMER?"

❀

Dentist: Ma'am, that tooth looks very bad. I'm going to have to pull it.

Patient: Get my tooth pulled? You've got to be kidding. I'd rather go through childbirth!

Dentist: Well, make up your mind. I have to adjust the chair.

❀

NON SEQUITUR • By Wiley

❀

Sign on a maternity-ward door:
Push! Push! Push!

❀

When your weight goes up and down and up and down, that's what's known as the rhythm method of girth control.

❀

I'm not fat. I'm a nutritional overachiever.

❀

"NOW I KNOW WHY PATSY CLAIRMONT SAYS MAMMOGRAM TECHNICIANS ARE LIKE MAGICIANS . . . THEY CAN TURN YOUR CUPS INTO SAUCERS!"

❀

I *am* in shape. Round is a shape.

❀

If we are what we eat,
then I'm easy, fast, and cheap.

❀

When asked what is the secret of a long and happy life, the Duchess of Windsor responded, "Fill what's empty, empty what's full, and scratch where it itches."[1]

❀

At ceremonies commemorating the hundredth anniversary of Harry S. Truman's birth, the White House counsel during the Truman Administration was reminiscing. He recalled being at a White House banquet one night when one of the guests turned to the woman seated next to him.

"Did I get your name correctly?" he asked. "Is your name Post?"

"Yes, I'm Emily Post," the woman answered.

"The world-renowned authority on manners?" the man asked.

"Well, yes, I guess you could say so," Mrs. Post said. "Why do you ask?"

"Because," the man answered, "you just ate my salad."[2]

❀

Never be afraid to try something new.

Remember: Amateurs built the ark. Professionals built the *Titanic*.

❀

Hang in there! In just two days
tomorrow will be yesterday.

❀

Guess what I lost this week...

My glasses.

❈

A recent news report said the typical symptoms of stress are eating too much, impulse buying, and driving too fast. Are they kidding? That's my idea of a perfect day!

❈

The best things are nearest: Breath in your nostrils, light in your eyes, flowers at your feet, duties at your hand, the path of God just before you.

—ROBERT LOUIS STEVENSON

❈

❀

Best time to be happy: *now.*
Best place to be happy: *here!*

❀

There are some days when I don't know whether life
is passing me by or trying to run me over.

❀

They're a perfect couple:
He's a hypochondriac, and she's a pill.

❀

May those who love us, love us;
And those who don't—may God turn
their hearts;
And if He doesn't turn their hearts,
may He turn their ankles
So we may know them by their limping.

❀

I can't cook, hate to clean, and loathe ironing. The only thing domestic about me is that I was born in this country.[3]

❀

**"OH, GLORY! OH, DELIGHT!
MY ESTROGEN PATCH JUST KICKED IN!"**

© 2003 Barbara Johnson

✿

I have a great diet. You're allowed to eat anything you want, but you must eat it in the company of naked fat people.

✿

The second day of a diet is always easier than the first. By the second day, you're off it.

✿

A preacher visited an elderly woman from his congregation. As he sat on the couch he noticed a bowl of peanuts on the coffee table. "Mind if I have a few?" he asked.

"No, not at all," the old woman replied.

They chatted for an hour, and as the preacher stood to leave, he realized he had emptied most of the bowl. "I'm so sorry for eating all your peanuts," he said. "I really just meant to eat a few."

"Oh, that's all right," replied the old woman. "Ever since I lost my teeth all I can do is suck the chocolate off them."

✿

My idea of a balanced diet: a cookie in each hand.

✿

The easiest way to lose weight is to check it as airline baggage.[4]

✿

© 1999 Randy Glasbergen.   www.glasbergen.com

"You'll lose weight on any strict diet, but it's mostly water...from crying."

❀

Diet Rule #1:
Never weigh more than your refrigerator.[5]

❀

We've reached that age where just haulin' our fat around counts as a workout.

❀

I like to think I'm at that stage Margaret Mead described as PMZ: Post-Menopausal Zest!

❀

The late Erma Bombeck said when she went to sign up for an exercise class, they told her to wear loose clothing.

"Who are you kidding?" asked Erma. "If I had any loose clothing I wouldn't need to take the class!"

❀

Chuck Swindoll said his children gave him a plaque that said:

> DIETS ARE FOR PEOPLE
> WHO ARE THICK—AND TIRED OF IT.

❀

> Can it be an accident that "STRESSED"
> is "DESSERTS" spelled backward?

❀

Your body is like a superbly engineered luxury automobile: If you use it wisely and maintain it properly . . . it will eventually break down anyway, most likely in a bad neighborhood.

—DAVE BARRY

❀

I refuse to think of them as chin hairs.
I think of them as stray eyebrows.

—JANETTE BARBER

❀

He who sits in the heavens laughs.

PSALM 2:4 NASB

❀

NON SEQUITUR By Wiley

When dieting, remember:

What's on the table eventually becomes what's on the chair.

❀

CLOSE TO HOME By John McPherson

Nellie tries out her miracle bra.

❀

It is bad to suppress laughter.

It goes back down and spreads to your hips.[6]

WHO ARE THESE KIDS,
AND WHY ARE THEY CALLING ME MOM?

*For **this** I have stretch marks?*

There is an evolution to becoming a mother. Once you become a parent it's like getting a life sentence with no hope of parole! And no matter how old we get, we mothers watch our kids—even when they're middle-aged—for signs of improvement. We're always hoping that something we instilled in them *might* show up.

Yes, becoming a parent changes everything, but parenthood itself also changes with each baby. For example, consider your wardrobe. As soon as the home pregnancy-test kit confirms that you're pregnant, you head for the mall—and come home wearing a maternity outfit.

With the second baby, you squeeze into your regular clothes as long as possible.

With the third baby, your maternity clothes ARE your regular clothes.

❀

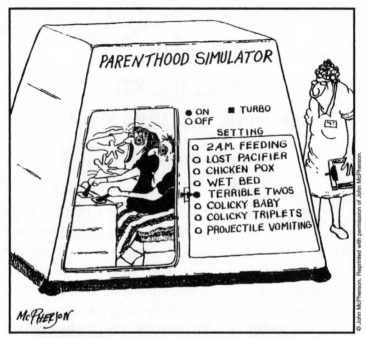

In an effort to prepare expectant parents for the challenges that lie ahead, many obstetricians' offices have installed parenthood simulators.

❀

We childproofed our home,
but they're still getting in.

❀

Raising kids is part joy and part guerrilla warfare.[1]

❀

A teenage boy was taking care of his baby sister while his parents went shopping. He decided to go fishing, so he had to take her along.

"I'll never do that again!" he told his mother that evening. "I didn't catch a thing!"

"Oh, next time I'm sure she'll be quiet and not scare the fish away," his mother said.

The boy answered, "It wasn't that. She ate all the bait."

❀

Youth:

By the time your face clears up,
your mind gets fuzzy.

❀

Chuck Swindoll recalled how, during their first week of parenthood, he and his wife realized that what they really had was not a child but a cross between *The Terminator* and *The Swamp Thing*. "I mean, this creature sleeps when you're awake and is wide awake when you're asleep, and has a set of lungs to drown out a Concorde jet," said Swindoll. "My wife used to say, 'Honey, I'm sort of forgetting what our baby's face looks like, I'm spending so much time at the other end.'"[2]

❀

I can see clearly now. My brain is gone.

❀

**What mothers think of when someone
suggests they can change the world.**

❀

New wonder drugs from modern medicine:

St. Mom's Wort—Plant extract that treats Mom's
exhaustion by rendering preschoolers unconscious for
up to six hours.

Empty-Nestrogen—Highly effective medication
that eliminates melancholy by enhancing memory of
how awful they were as teenagers and how you
couldn't wait 'til they moved out.

❀

One exhausted young mother of three rambunctious pre-schoolers was asked whether she would have children if she had it to do all over again.

"Sure," she responded, "just not the same ones."

❀

If you have a lot of tension and you get a headache, do what it says on the aspirin bottle: "Take two aspirin" and "Keep away from children."

❀

"That better not be my Christmas present!"

❀

Preparing for Parenthood

If you're wondering whether you have what it takes to be a parent, here's a little list of preparations to help you get ready for the blessed event:

Mother's Preparation for Pregnancy: From the food co-op, obtain a twenty-five-pound bag of pinto beans. Attach it to your waist with a belt. Wear it everywhere you go for nine months. Then remove ten beans to indicate the baby has been born.

Mess-Management Preparation: Smear grape jelly on the living room furniture and curtains. Now plunge your hands into a bag of potting soil, wipe them on the walls, and highlight the smudges with Magic Markers.

Inhalation Therapy Preparation: Empty a carton of milk onto the cloth upholstery of the family car, park the vehicle in a sunny spot, then leave it to ripen for the month of August. Open the door and breathe deeply.

Shopping Preparation: Herd a flock of goats through the grocery store. Always keep every goat in sight and bring enough money to pay for whatever they eat or destroy.

Financial Preparation: Arrange for the family's paycheck to be split equally between the nearest grocery store and the pediatrician's office for the next two decades.

Aerobic-Agility Preparation: Try to dress the family cat in a small pantsuit complete with button shirt, snap-leg pants, lace-up shoes, and a bow tie while the neighbor's German shepherd barks out encouragement from two feet away. (Make sure paramedics are standing by.)

❊

Two things every mom needs:
Velcro arms and a Teflon heart.

❊

© 1997 Randy Glasbergen. www.glasbergen.com

GLASBERGEN

"Let's try getting up every night at 2:00 AM to feed the cat. If we enjoy doing that, then we can talk about having a baby."

❊

THE FAMILY CIRCUS.   **By Bil Keane**

"I know why the car pool's so late, Mommy! This
is OUR morning to drive!"

❄

My nerves are a-twitter; my hair has gone white.
My knees, they are knocking; I'm quaking
    with fright.
My whole life is streaking in front of my eyes.
"Dear Lord, please be with me!" I urgently cry.
My heart's in my throat, but at least I'm alive.
The problem? I'm teaching my kid how to drive!

—ANN LUNA

❄

Things moms would probably never say:

- "How can you see the TV sitting so far back?"
- "Sure, you can miss school today. I used to skip school a lot, too."
- "Just leave all the lights on. We have extra money this month for the bill."
- "Let me smell that shirt. Yeah, that's good for another week."
- "Well, if Timmy's mom says it's okay, that's good enough for me!"
- "I don't have a tissue with me . . . just wipe your nose on your sleeve."
- "Don't bother wearing a jacket. The wind chill is bound to improve."

❀

A teacher asked her Sunday school class to draw pictures of their favorite Bible stories. She was puzzled by Jimmy's picture, which showed four people on an airplane. She asked him what story he meant.

"The flight to Egypt," Jimmy said.

"I see. Mary, Joseph, and Baby Jesus," the teacher answered. "But who's the fourth person?"

"Oh, that's Pontius—the pilot!"

❀

Happiness is having a large, loving, caring, close-knit family . . . in another city.[3]

THE FAMILY CIRCUS ®   By Bil Keane

"I'm grounded. I said one more word
to my mother."

More truths brought to us by children:
- Don't let your mom brush your hair when she's mad at your dad.
- If your sister hits you, don't hit her back. It's always the second person who gets caught.
- Never hold the cat while the vacuum cleaner is running.
- When you're in trouble the best place to be is in Grandma's lap.

❀

I note with great interest that when God made the first human being, Adam, He created him as a complete adult and thus totally bypassed diapers, colic, toddlerhood, adolescence, and driving lessons. . . .

My personal theory is that God designed parenthood, in part, as an enormous character-building exercise, and since God does not personally require character improvement, He didn't need to bother getting Adam to eat strained peas.[4]

❀

After putting her children to bed, a mother changed into old slacks and a droopy blouse and then washed her hair in the sink and smeared her face with a slick, green moisturizing cream that hardened into a mask. As she heard the children getting more and more rambunctious, her patience evaporated. At last she threw a towel around her dripping hair and stormed into their room, threatening all sorts of dire punishments if they didn't get back into bed and go to sleep.

As she left the room, she heard a small voice whisper in the darkness, "Who *was* that?"

❀

Raising teenagers is like
nailing Jell-O to the wall.

❀

"O.K., Sweeties. You're all going to need to go naked for just a day or two till Mommy catches up with the laundry."

❁

If you want to be loved,
don't criticize those you want to love you.[5]

❁

Kids are like sponges.
They absorb all your strength and leave you limp.
Give 'em a squeeze, and you get it all back.

❁

A mother watched as her daughter hopped off the school bus and scampered toward her house in a pouring rainstorm. As the little girl ran toward the house, a lightning bolt flashed and the little girl stopped, looked up toward the sky and smiled, then began running back toward the house.

Another lightning bolt flashed, and again the little girl stopped, looked toward the sky, and smiled before running once more toward the open door of her house.

When the little girl finally arrived in the house, her mother immediately asked about her strange behavior. "Why did you keep stopping and smiling at the sky?" she asked her daughter.

"I had to, Mommy," the little girl explained. "God was taking my picture."

❀

When my granddaughter Kandee was five years old, I took her with me while I was speaking at a conference. During praise time, the words to the songs were displayed on a big screen, and I was surprised to see little Kandee enthusiastically singing each and every song. I knew she couldn't read yet, and I was impressed that she knew all the words by heart. Later when I complimented her on knowing so many songs, she said, "Oh, Grandma Barb, I didn't know any of those songs. I just sing 'watermelon–peanut butter,' and it all comes out right!"

❀

CALVIN and HOBBES By Bill Watterson

❀

A father gave his little girl a puppy for her birthday. Just an hour later he found a puddle in the middle of the kitchen floor.

The man called out for his daughter, who came running into the kitchen, and asked her to explain why she wasn't watching her new pet.

She looked at the puddle then looked up at her dad and said, "My pup runneth over."

❀

The opera house was sold out in anticipation of a world-famous singer's performance there. But when the lights dimmed, an announcement brought a groan from the crowd: "Ladies and gentlemen, we apologize for any disappointment this announcement may cause. Our featured singer has suffered a minor accident and will be unable to perform tonight. We hope you will welcome his understudy warmly."

The crowd muttered and sighed, and the opera began. The stand-in artist gave the performance everything he had. Throughout the evening, there had been nothing but an uneasy silence in the audience. Even at the end, no one applauded.

Then, from the balcony, the thin voice of a little girl broke the silence. "Daddy," she called out, "I think you were wonderful!"

The crowd broke into thunderous applause.[6]

❀

The sole purpose of a child's middle name
is so he can tell when he's really in trouble.

"Mother . . . please tell me this isn't you in these hideous bell-bottoms."

THREE STAGES OF LIFE: YOUTH, MATURITY, AND "MY, YOU'RE LOOKIN' GOOD!"

At my age, I've found that going bra-less pulls all the wrinkles out of my face

According to my birth certificate, I'm living somewhere between estrogen and death, or, as someone said, between menopause and LARGE PRINT! But I don't have to act my age because, thank God, I've discovered a wonderful antiaging remedy. It won't actually turn back the clock, and it's certainly nothing new. In fact it's been promoted since biblical times as a cure for a wide variety of problems (see Proverbs 17:22). And it's no secret, either; lots of people use it.

What is this miraculous wonder-worker?

Laughter. A sense of humor. An attitude expressed by Oscar Wilde's motto: "Life is too important to be taken seriously."

Come on. Turn the page. Life is happening, and we've got some important laughing to do.

❀

DEAR BARBARA: Lately I have had real fears that I may be going off my rocker. How can I know if this is what is happening to me?

—FEARFUL IN FAYETTEVILLE

DEAR FEARFUL: We know that one out of every four people in this country is mentally unbalanced. So you just think of your three closest friends . . . and if they seem to be okay, then you're the one!

DEAR BARBARA: A friend of mine who is only fifty years old tells people she is sixty, because she looks GREAT for sixty but AWFUL for fifty. Should I tell her I know she is lying?

—PEEVED IN PODUNK

DEAR PEEVED: There are a couple of Scripture verses on lies that I get twisted up sometimes . . . but I think it goes like this: A lie is an abomination to the Lord, but an ever-present help in time of trouble! Just encourage your friend by reminding her that some people never lose their beauty; they merely move it from their faces into their hearts.

❀

You can judge your age by the amount of pain you feel when you come in contact with a new idea.

❀

Real Life Adventures by Gary Wise and Lance Aldrich

The first time you're offered a senior citizen discount.

❀

I don't know what it's like to be old, but I think it's living long enough to make a joke of the things that once broke your heart.

❀

It may be true that life begins at forty, but that's also when everything else begins to wear out, fall out, or spread out.

❀

The older you get, the tougher it is to lose weight, because by then your body and your fat are really good friends.

❀

The only way to look younger is
not to be born so soon.

❀

Courtroom lawyer, questioning a potential juror:
Q: Have you lived in this town all your life?
A: Not yet!

❀

A feeble, elderly woman, all hunched up and using a cane, limped into a doctor's office. Five minutes later, she came out walking erect and without a limp.

A man in the waiting room asked, "Gee, what did the doc do? You're doing great now."

The lady replied, "He gave me a longer cane."

❀

Those who love deeply never grow old;
they may die of old age, but they die young.[1]

❀

If you want long friendships, develop a short memory.[2]

❀

❀

Over the years, I've learned who is my friend and who is NOT my friend.

GRAVITY is NOT my friend!

❀

When you're old, the challenge is not in bending down to touch your toes.

It's remembering what you're there for once you arrive.

❀

Stop the Conspiracy!

Have you noticed that when you're over the hill, everything seems *uphill* from where you are? Stairs are steeper. Groceries are heavier. And *everything* is farther away. Yesterday I walked to the corner and was dumbfounded to discover how long our street had become.

And that's not all. People are less considerate now, especially the younger ones. They speak in whispers all the time, and if you ask them to speak up, they just repeat themselves, endlessly mouthing the same silent message until they're red in the face and exhausted. What do they think I am, a lipreader?

And they drive so fast you're risking life and limb if you happen to pull onto the freeway in front of them. All I can say is, their brakes must wear out awfully fast, the way I see them screech and swerve in my rearview mirror.

Even clothing manufacturers are becoming less civilized these days. Why else would they suddenly start labeling a size 6 dress as a 12? Do they think no one notices that these things no longer fit around the waist, hips, thighs, and bosom?

The people who make bathroom scales are pulling the same prank but in reverse. Do they think I actually *believe* the number I see on that dial? Ha! I would never let myself weigh that much!

Just who do these people think they're fooling? I'd like to call up someone in authority to report what's going on—but the telephone company is in on the conspiracy. They've printed the phone books in such small type that no one could ever find a number there!

All I can do is pass along this warning: Maturity is under attack! Unless something drastic happens, pretty soon *everyone* will have to suffer these awful indignities.

❀

**"I've reached the age where
I need three pairs of glasses:
one for driving, one for reading—
and one to find the other two!"**

❀

I've reached that point in life where
the only thing I can exercise is CAUTION!

❀

Great news: Laughing heartily one hundred times is the physiological equivalent to working out on a rowing machine for ten minutes. The problem is, once I get going, I'm afraid I won't be able to stop, and I'll laugh myself into anorexia![3]

❀

There are two kinds of women who will pay big bucks for a makeup mirror that magnifies their faces. The first ones are young models who need to be sure to cover every eyelash and define their lips. The second group are women who, without their glasses, can't even *find* their faces.

❀

Do you ever have those mornings when you wake up and feel like your get-up-and-go has already got up and gone?

❀

You know you're getting old when you make mental notes to yourself . . . and then forget where you put them.

❀

After a certain age, if you don't wake up aching in every joint you are probably dead.

❀

I have a friend who has a magical way of finding humor in every situation. Recently she wrote me a note that said, "My friend Irene is *always* complaining! I took her to a greeting-card store the other day, and she looked and looked and looked.

"Finally I said, 'Irene, what in the world are you looking for?'

"She replied, 'I'm looking for a card that says, "I had what you've got—only WORSE!"'"

This is the same witty woman who told me her horoscope predicted one morning that she was going to have an adventure involving water. "And then," she continued, "I dropped my false teeth in the toilet!"

❊

"Having nine lives is cool, but if I have to go through menopause again, forget it!"

❀

With age a woman gains wisdom,
maturity, self-assurance . . .
and ten pounds right on the hips.[4]

❀

Age gracefully? I think not! Age ferociously instead. Seize everything valuable within reach. Extend. Question. Give. The face will follow. All the cosmetic surgeons in the world could never produce such a face.[5]

❀

A favorite game of aging pranksters:
Sag—you're it!

❀

One jokester said you know you're getting old when you start adapting those blessed old hymns of days gone by, especially

- "Go Tell It on the Mountain—and Speak Up!"
- "Nobody Knows the Trouble I Have Seeing"
- "Guide Me, O Thou Great Jehovah (I've Forgotten Where I Parked)"

❀

Recipe for aging fearlessly: Lay your worries aside, fill your heart with the comfort of God's love and mercy—and find something to laugh about!

❀

Author Max Lucado said he received these happy birthday wishes when he turned forty:

- You know you're getting older when you try to straighten out the wrinkles in your socks only to find you aren't wearing any.
- At twenty we don't care what the world thinks of us; at thirty we start to worry about what the world thinks of us; at forty we realize the world isn't thinking of us at all.
- I've gotten to the age where I need my false teeth and hearing aid before I can ask where I left my glasses.
- Forty is when you stop patting yourself on the back and start patting yourself under the chin.[6]

❁

There are many women like me who talk about cosmetic surgery, but our philosophy prevails:

No guts—live with the ruts.

❁

Despite the high cost of living,
have you noticed how it remains so popular?

❁

Bumper sticker:
I intend to live forever.
So far, so good.

❁

GOD IS ONE OF
THE ELDERLY

ED FISCHER

❁

Midlife is when you can stand naked in front of a
mirror and see your rear end without turning around.

❁

I'm at that age where the memory starts to go. In
fact, these days the only thing I can retain is water.

❁

"I'm approaching the age of 30."
"Really? From which direction?"[7]

❁

A greeting-card verse we'll probably never see:
You had your bladder removed,
now you're on the mend.
Here's a bouquet of flowers
and a box of Depends.

❀

A telephone greeting I hope I never hear:
"Thank you for calling the Incontinence Hotline.
Can you hold please?"

❀

A woman went to her doctor to get the results of some medical tests. The doctor said, "I have good news and bad news. Which do you want first?"

She answered, "The good news."

He said, "You have twenty-four hours to live."

"Good grief!" exclaimed the woman. "That's the *good* news? Then what's the *bad* news?"

"I was supposed to tell you yesterday."

❀

It's pretty hard to say what *does* bring happiness.
Poverty and wealth have both failed.[8]

❀

Errors have been made. Others will be blamed.

❀

Expectations = Premeditated Resentment

❀

My body is all messed up. My nose runs, and my feet smell.

❀

Mixed maxims:
Don't count your chickens before they cross the road.
He who laughs first shall be last.
Beauty is only skin deep . . . in the eye of the beholder.[9]

❀

© 1987 by Mary McBride. Reprinted from *Grandma Knows Best,
but No One Ever Listens!* with permission of Meadowbrook Press.

IF IT WEREN'T FOR MEN . . .
WHAT WOULD THERE BE TO LAUGH ABOUT?

Men are like parking spaces.
All the good ones are already taken—
and the rest are handicapped or
their meters are running out!

While I was recovering from my adventure with a malignant brain tumor, my husband, Bill, was my full-time helper—and occasionally my headache! For six months after my surgery, he never left me alone for more than an hour or so at a time while he made quick trips out to the post office, the bank, the grocery store, and the pharmacy.

During those stressful times he tended to my every need, sorting the dozens of pills I had to take every day into a big muffin tin and making sure I took the precise dose at the precise time around the clock. Knowing what a scatterbrain I can be, my doctor flat-out told me at the end of the summer that my survival was directly due to Bill's diligence in ensuring that I had followed the detailed regimen of medication that had been ordered for me. That is why I say right up front that Bill saved my life. It's also why I sometimes refer to him as Mr. Headache.

Bill was an ace fighter pilot during World War II—and today he drives like he's still in pursuit of those enemy attackers. Because I have a low tolerance for terror, for years Bill let me drive whenever we would go somewhere together. But during my recovery, he had to do the driving, and there were times when he delivered me to the chemo clinic or the doctor's office with blood pressure high enough to power the geysers at Yellowstone.

And then there was the grocery shopping. Being very frugal (*tight* is the word!), Bill loves a bargain— whether or not it's something we actually like to eat. One day early in my treatment my doctor told me, "Barb, your priority right now is to get well. So I'm giving you a new prescription. It's a prescription for rest. I want you to get plenty of rest and only do the things you really enjoy doing. Just do what *you* want to do— your favorite things. That's *all* you're allowed to do."

Empowered by the doctor's directive, I went right home and did something wild and wonderful—something I *really* wanted to do. I marched resolutely into the kitchen, found the industrial-sized box of boring cereal

Bill had brought home from the warehouse club, and dumped it in the trash. Unfortunately, Bill rounded the kitchen corner just as the last flake was fluttering into the trash can.

"What are you doing?" he asked, eyes wide, eyebrows lifted.

"The doctor told me to do it," I answered.

"He told you to pour out a perfectly good box of cereal?"

"He told me to do whatever I wanted to do for the next few weeks while I get ready for the chemo. You bought this fifty-five-gallon drum of cereal at the warehouse club, and I've never liked it. I'll be dead before I eat it all, Bill. I don't like it, and I don't want to eat it, and the doctor told me to do anything I wanted, and *this* is what I decided I wanted to do. So I did it," I stated emphatically, folding my arms for emphasis and catching a glimpse of my determined image reflected in the door of the microwave. My head, still mostly bald from the brain surgery I'd just gone through, was gleaming under the kitchen light. (It's so hard to be dignified when your scalp is glowing like a streetlight.)

"Oh, brother!" Bill muttered and headed out the door.

You might have thought Bill would catch on and be a little more discerning in his purchases after that, but he still gets the most joy out of buying whatever's cheapest. As the year went on, I had to call my friends whose birthdays were coming up and warn them that Bill would be picking out the birthday cards we would be mailing them. "So if you get a card that says, 'Get well soon' or 'Sorry for your loss,' you'll know he bought the ones that were on sale," I told them.

Bill's occasionally my headache. But he makes up for his contrariness by being a very low-maintenance kind of guy. After all he had done to take care of me during the cancer crisis, when his birthday neared I told him I wanted to do something really special for him to show him how much I appreciated him.

"So . . . what would you like to do to celebrate?" I asked him. "And what's a special gift I can get you to let you know how much I appreciate all you've done to help during my illness?"

He didn't even hesitate. "I'd like to go to Price Club and get a hotdog."

I should have known. For Bill, there are only two food groups: hotdogs and popcorn. And, being a connoisseur of hotdogs, Bill has decided the hotdogs served in the snack bar at Price Club are the world's best. So off we went to the big store.

Sharing our hotdog lunch in the cavernous building, I couldn't help but think how easy Bill is to love and how good he has been to me (not to mention how easy it is to shop for his birthday!).

As we sat there munching our hotdogs, I remembered another time when a favorite food created a special moment for Bill and me. Several years ago my publisher notified me that sales of my books had topped the one-million mark and offered to fly Bill and me to its head-quarters to celebrate with a party. Neither Bill nor I wanted that kind of attention; instead, Bill called our publishing friends, thanked them for their offer, and told them we would do something special on our own. Then he headed for the door. "I'll be back in a little while," he called over his shoulder.

While he was gone I imagined him out there shop-ping for some unique little gift or setting up a special outing to celebrate this milestone. Maybe he was arrang-ing a dinner party at our favorite restaurant. Maybe he was putting together a little train trip to a scenic place, something we'd always enjoyed doing. *Or,* I mused, *jewelry would be nice.*

Pretty soon he was back. I met him at the door with a wide smile, eager to see what he had brought. The mystery item was in a brown grocery sack, which he dropped onto the kitchen table with a thud.

"I got you some fresh asparagus—white asparagus," he said with a proud grin.

"*Asparagus?*" I answered, not sure I'd understood.

"I know how you like it," he said sweetly.

We celebrated that evening with a simple little dinner (which I cooked, of course) featuring my favorite food, fresh white asparagus. And we had a fine time. It wasn't what I'd been expecting from Bill, but, being an only child, he has always been a bit odd, and I've grown rather fond of his strange ways. Being married to him all these years has been quite an experience, a thrilling adventure filled with shared love and heartache, hotdogs and asparagus. And popcorn. *Lots* and *lots* of popcorn. Bill has been the strong shoulder I've leaned on—and the silly source of lots of laughter. In fact, he has served as my launch pad for a treasure trove of humor hidden in the antics and actions of the opposite sex. In this chapter, I'm glad to share some of my favorites.

❁

A new bride moved in with her husband. She put a shoebox on a shelf and asked him never to touch it. For fifty years the man left the box alone until his wife was old and dying. As he was putting her affairs in order, he found the box and thought it might hold something important. Inside he found two doilies and twenty-five hundred dollars in cash. Curious, he asked his wife about the contents.

"My mother gave me that box the day we married," she said. "She told me to make a doily to ease my frustrations every time I got mad at you."

The husband was touched that in fifty years she'd been mad at him only twice.

"But what's the money for?" he asked.

"Oh," she answered, "that's the money I made selling the doilies."[1]

A greeting-card verse only a man would send:
My tire was thumping; I thought it was flat;
When I looked at the tire, I noticed your cat. Sorry!

❀

Men have three basic hair styles:
parted, unparted, and departed!

❀

One of my friends who is bald says he will *never* wear a turtleneck sweater. He's afraid he'll look like a roll-on deodorant!

This is the same friend who said he used to use Head & Shoulders—but now he needs Mop & Glo.

❀

Cure for Baldness in Men
Combine Epsom salts, persimmon juice, and alum; form a paste and rub mixture on head daily. (It won't keep your hair from falling out, but it shrinks your head to fit what you have left.)

❀

In his book *In the Grip of Grace*, author and pastor Max Lucado says he used to be a "closet slob" with the attitude, "Life is too short to match our socks; just buy longer pants!" Then, he says, he got married!

❀

Wise husbands know that PMS is Mother Nature's way of saying, "Get out of the house!"

❀

After a canceled flight, anxious passengers mobbed the ticket counter. The airline agents were doing their best to rebook passengers quickly, but a demanding passenger pushed to the front of the line, pounded on the counter, and shouted repeatedly, "You *have* to get me on this plane!"

The agent remained accommodating and unrattled, but the passenger became even more incensed and insulting. "Do you know who you're talking to?" he shouted. "Do you know who I am?"

The agent calmly took the microphone and announced over the intercom, "Ladies and gentlemen, we have a passenger here who doesn't know who he is. Will someone who knows this passenger please come identify him?"

With that, the other passengers broke into applause.[2]

❀

This is a rule for women that has no exceptions:
If it has tires or testosterone,
you're gonna have trouble with it.

❀

One man's definition of the term "mixed emotions":
Watching your mother-in-law drive off a cliff in your new Cadillac.

❀

IF WOMEN CONTROLLED MEDICINE

❀

When I die, I want to go peacefully, like my grandfather did—in his sleep. Not screaming, like the passengers in his car.

❀

Man trying to meet woman: "Hey, sweetie, what's your sign?"

Woman: "Do not enter."

❀

Q: How would you make a marriage work?
A: Tell your wife she looks pretty even if she looks like a truck.

—RICKY, AGE TEN

❀

Never criticize your spouse's faults;
if it weren't for them, your mate might have found someone better than you![3]

❀

A joke:

Do old men wear boxers or briefs?
Depends!

❀

There are two theories for arguing with a woman. Neither one works.

❀

Tell a man there are four hundred billion stars, and he'll believe you. Tell him a bench has wet paint, and he just has to touch it.

—STEVEN WRIGHT

❀

Dads know there are three ways to get something done:
1. Do it yourself.
2. Hire someone to do it.
3. Forbid your kids to do it.

❀

A young man came to a family reunion with extremely red ears. He explained that he had been intently watching the championship football game on TV. His wife was standing near his chair, doing the ironing, and she had set the phone on the ironing board so she could talk to her mother while she worked. When she left to hang the ironed clothes in the closet, the phone rang.

"I was deeply engrossed in the game at that point," the man said. "So, keeping my eyes glued to the television, I reached for the phone but grabbed the hot iron and put it to my ear."

"But how did *both* ears get burned?" someone asked.

"I hadn't any more than hung up," the man said, "when the guy called back!"

"No, dear. The phone's working fine — you just answered the TV remote."

© 2003 Barbara Johnson

"I'm always losing my car keys,
my temper, my memory and my patience...
so losing weight should be a breeze!"

❀

I love this list a friend sent me off the Internet, show-
ing classes for men offered at a community's learning
center:

Topic 1: How to Fill Up the Ice Trays. Step-by-step
instructions with slide presentation.

Topic 2: The Toilet Paper Roll—Does It Grow on
the Holder? Round-table discussion.

Topic 3: Fundamental Differences between the
Laundry Hamper and the Floor. Photos and explanatory
graphics will be shown.

Topic 4: Learning How to Find Things, Starting
with Looking in the Right Place Instead of Turning the
House Upside Down While Screaming. Open forum.

© 1997 Randy Glasbergen.

GLASBERGEN

**"I made you a doctor appointment.
On Friday morning you're going in
to have your frown removed."**

❀

Sign on a plumber's truck:
We repair what your husband fixed.

❀

Bumper sticker on a man's car:
DRIVER CARRIES NO CASH.
(HE'S MARRIED.)

❀

Only two things are necessary to keep one's
wife happy. One is to let her think she is having
her own way. The other is to let her have it.

—LYNDON JOHNSON

6

LAUGH, I THOUGHT I'D DIE!

*Being tickled to death
is a great way to live*

As Christians we have a distinct advantage over nonbelievers: We don't have to be afraid of dying. We know that our final exit here will be our grandest entrance there—in heaven. We know exactly where we're going, and we're eager to get there. That means we can laugh at death—and that's just what we'll do in this chapter!

❀

"If I sold my house and my car, had a big garage sale, and gave all my money to the church, would that get me into heaven?" the Sunday school teacher asked her class.

"No-o-o-o-o!" the youngsters answered in unison.

"If I cleaned the church every day, mowed the yard, and kept everything neat and tidy, would that get me into heaven?"

"No-o-o-o-o!" came the answer again.

"Well, then, if I am kind to animals and give candy

to all the children, and love my family, would that get me into heaven?" she asked again.

"No-o-o-o-o-o!" they all agreed.

"Well, then how *can* I get into heaven?" she asked.

A five-year-old boy shouted, "You gotta be DEAD!"

❊

"Well, the doctors were right—they said I'd
be out of the hospital within a couple of weeks."

❊

There's nothing discreditable in dying. I have known the most respectable people to do it.

—C. S. LEWIS

❊

Death is the golden key
that opens the palace of eternity.

—MILTON

I have no idea when Jesus is coming back.

I'm on the Welcoming Committee, not the Planning Committee.[1]

❀

The young man was at the end of his rope. Seeing no way out, he dropped to his knees in prayer. "Lord, I can't go on," he said. "I have too heavy a cross to bear."

The Lord replied, "My son, if you can't bear its weight, just place your cross inside this room. Then pick out any cross you wish."

The man was filled with relief. "Thank You, Lord!" he sighed, and he did as he was told.

Inside the room, he saw many crosses, some so large the tops weren't visible. Then he spotted a tiny cross leaning against a far wall.

"I'd like that one, Lord," he whispered.

"My son," the Lord replied, "that's the cross you just brought in."

❀

Riddle:
What's gray, crispy, and hangs from the ceiling?
An amateur electrician.[2]

❀

Epitaph over a dentist's grave:
He is filling his last cavity.[3]

❀

NON SEQUITUR By Wiley

I've come to realize that most of the things I worry about never happen—which just proves that worry *does* work!

❀

Live each day as if it were your last.
Someday you'll be right.

❀

On Valentine's Day a wrinkled old man sat on the bus seat holding a bunch of fresh roses. Across the aisle was a young girl whose sad eyes seemed to be locked on the floor—except for moments when she glanced back again and again at the man's flowers.

The time came for the old man to get off. Impulsively he thrust the flowers into the girl's lap. "I can see you love the roses," he explained. "I was taking them to my wife, but I know she would like for you to have them. I'll tell her I gave them to you."

The girl accepted the flowers with a delighted smile then watched the old man get off the bus . . . and walk through the gate of a cemetery.

❀

The way to heaven:
Turn right at Calvary and keep going straight!

❀

Death is God's way of telling you,
"Your table is ready."

❀

"I would have been here sooner,
but I got hooked on oat bran muffins."

❀

There was a great loss today in the entertainment world. The man who wrote the song "Hokey Pokey" died. What was really horrible is that they had trouble keeping the body in the casket. They'd put his right leg in and . . . well, you know the rest.[4]

❀

A mother asked her daughter, "Did you say your prayers last night?"

The little girl answered, "Well, I got down on my knees and started to say them, and all of a sudden I thought, *I bet God gets awfully tired of hearing the same old prayer over and over.* So I crawled into bed and told Him the story of the three bears."[5]

❀

Two ninety-year-old men, Herb and Herman, were at the funeral service for another ninety-year-old pal. After the benediction, they lingered, looking at the open casket of the deceased friend. Finally, Herb said to Herman, "You know, it's hardly worth going home."[6]

❀

Some of the best excuses for laughing at death come from the tabloid headlines on display in the grocery store checkout line. Here are some of my favorites:

- Bolt of Lightning Turns Toilet into Electric Chair
- Nearsighted Hubby Scared to Death by Wife's Wig—Thought It Was a Rat!
- Preacher Goes Nuts and Drowns Woman during River Baptism
- Dead Man's Heart Started with Jumper Cables—Quick-Thinking Mechanic Brings Victim Back to Life

❀

"I'm getting so old that all my friends in heaven
will think I didn't make it."

❀

Enjoy what *is* . . . before it *isn't*.

❀

If in the last year you haven't discarded a major
opinion or acquired a new one, check your pulse. You
may be dead!

❀

A woman was dying. A pastor was summoned, and he attempted to comfort her, but to no avail. "I am lost," she said. "I have ruined my life and every life around me. Now I'm going painfully to hell. There is no hope for me."

The pastor saw a framed picture of a pretty girl on the dresser. "Who is this?" he asked. The pale woman brightened. "She's my daughter, the one beautiful thing in my life."

"And would you help her if she were in trouble or made a mistake? Would you forgive her? Would you still love her?"

"Of course I would!" cried the woman. "I would do anything for her! Why do you ask such a question?"

"Because I want you to know," said the pastor, "that God has a picture of you on His dresser."[7]

❀

Engraved on the tombstone
of the mother of nine children:
Here Lies Mom.
Let 'er R.I.P.

❀

Each of us can decrease the suffering of the world by adding to its joy.

—Dawn Markova

❀

HONK IF YOU THINK YOU'VE LIVED LONG ENOUGH!

❀

A woman leaned over my book table at a Women of Faith conference and whispered to me, "Barbara, your book saved my daughter's life."

Because it's more common to have mothers read my books than daughters, I said to the woman, "Oh? Your daughter read my book?"

"No," the woman answered. "*I* read it—and it kept me from killing her!"

❀

The three stages of life:

1. You *believe* in Santa Claus.
2. You *are* Santa Claus.
3. You *look* like Santa Claus.

❀

If you treat every situation as a life-and-death matter . . .
you will die a lot.

❀

Dear God,
Help me to bridle my tongue,
so that on Judgment Day
I will not be found guilty
of assault with a deadly weapon.

❀

Do you know how you can tell if you are co-dependent?

When you're dying, you see someone else's life pass before your eyes!

❀

Probably the only great thing about pantyhose is that every time you wash them they go back to their original shape. I look at that puckered, starved, withered six inches of nylon and feel reborn. God has given me a second chance to pack it in.

❀

The more you complain, the longer God lets you live.

❀

Life is for service. We human beings are meant to be helpers. In fact, the greatest thing we can do in life is to help our neighbors come to know that they are lovable and capable of loving. Anyone who truly knows this will not lose hope.

—FRED ROGERS

❀

Thanks for helping me over the hump!

© 2003 Barbara Johnson

NOTES

Chapter 1. Humor Comes at a Cost. Please Have Exact Change

1. Lowell D. Streiker, *Nelson's Big Book of Laughter* (Nashville: Thomas Nelson, 2000), 5.

2. Patty Wooten, R.N., *Heart, Humor, and Healing* (Mount Shasta, Calif.: Commune-a-Key, 1994).

3. *The Prairie Home Companion Pretty Good Joke Book*, vol. 3 (Minneapolis: Minnesota Public Radio, 1998), 3.

4. From Judy Garnatz Harriman's "Action" column in the *St. Petersburg (Fla.) Times*, 2 April 1995. Copyright 1995, *St. Petersburg Times*.

5. Adapted from Lowell D. Streiker, comp., *An Encyclopedia of Humor* (Peabody, Mass.: Hendrickson, 1998), 56.

6. "Bessie and Beulah," quoted in Streiker, *An Encyclopedia of Humor*, 235.

7. David Nicholas, quoted in *Draper's Book of Quotations for the Christian World* (Wheaton, Ill.: Tyndale, 1992), 9323.

Chapter 2. I Finally Got My Head Together—Then My Body Fell Apart

1. Streiker, *An Encyclopedia of Humor*, 188.

2. Adapted from Rob Gilbert, ed., *More of the Best of Bits & Pieces* (Fairfield, N.J.: Economics Press, 1997), 15.

3. Phyllis Diller, quoted in Roz Warren, ed., *Women's Lip* (Naperville, Ill.: Sourcebooks, 1999), 53.

4. Adapted from Peggy Ryan, quoted in Warren, *Women's Lip*, 24.

5. This little quip appeared on—what else?—a refrigerator magnet by Linda Grayson, produced by Printwick Papers.

6. Fred Allen, quoted by John and Anne Murphy in *The Laughter Prescription*, Summer 1994.

Chapter 3. Who Are These Kids, and Why Are They Calling Me Mom?

1. Ed Asner, quoted in *Reader's Digest*, February 2000, 69.

2. Chuck Swindoll, *The Tale of the Tardy Oxcart and 1,501 Other Stories* (Nashville: Word, 1998), 72.

3. George Burns, quoted in Streiker, *An Encyclopedia of Humor*, 121.

4. Dave Meurer, *Boyhood Daze: An Incomplete Guide to Raising Boys* (Minneapolis: Bethany House, 1999), 13.

5. Charles L. Allen, *Grandparents R Great* (Uhrichsville, Ohio: Barbour, 1992), 60.

6. Adapted from Arthur F. Lenehan, comp. and ed., *The Best of Bits & Pieces* (Fairfield, N.J.: Economics Press, 1994), 122.

Chapter 4. Three Stages of Life: Youth, Maturity, and "My, You're Lookin' Good!"

1. English playwright Sir Arthur Wing Pinero.

2. Gilbert, *More of the Best of Bits and Pieces*, 75.

3. Stanford University School of Medicine Psychiatrist William F. Fry, cited in "Fit Notes," *Tampa Tribune* Food and Health section, 14 November 1996, 6.

4. Rob Scott and Mike Wallard, designers, *Girls Just Wanna Have Facelifts: The Ugly Truth about Getting Older* (Kansas City: Shoebox Greetings, 1989).

5. Roger Rosenblatt, "Secret Admirer," *Modern Maturity,* August 1993.

6. Max Lucado, *A Gentle Thunder* (Nashville: Word, 1995), 60.

7. Bob Phillips, *Bob Phillips' Encyclopedia of Good Clean Jokes* (Eugene, Oreg.: Harvest House, 1992), 11.

8. Charlie "T." Jones and Bob Phillips, *Wit & Wisdom* (Eugene, Oreg: Harvest House, 1977), 109.

9. Diane Crosby, quoted in Streiker, *Nelson's Big Book of Laughter,* 265.

Chapter 5. If It Weren't for Men . . . What Would There Be to Laugh About?

1. Reprinted from the *Kansas City Star,* 29 October 2002.

2. Adapted from the *Tampa Tribune*, 25 June 1996, Baylife 2.

3. Jay Trachman, quoted in *Reader's Digest,* June 2000, 129.

Chapter 6. Laugh, I Thought I'd Die!

1. Tony Campolo, quoted in *A-Z Sparkling Illustrations,* comp. Stephen Gaukroger and Nick Mercer (Grand Rapids: Baker, 1997), 114.

2. Doc Blakely, "Laughter, the Best Medicine," *Reader's Digest,* August 1999, 89.

3. *The Last Word: Tombstone Wit and Wisdom,* comp. Nicola Gillies (Oxford, England: Dove Tail Books, 1997).

4. Adapted from Streiker, *Nelson's Big Book of Laughter,* 119.

5. Ibid.

6. Reggie the Retiree, *Laughs and Limericks on Aging—in Large Print* (Fort Myers, Fla.: Reggie the Retiree Co., 1991).

7. *The Jokesmith,* quoted in Gilbert, *More of the Best of Bits & Pieces*, 73–74.